Slide Guitar Collection

25 Great Tunes for Slide Guitar

Arranged by Brent Robitaille

CONTENTS - SLIDE GUITAR COLLECTION

25 GREAT TUNES

EXERCISES - NOTE CHARTS – KLM

Slide Guitar Collection

Introduction

A good way to learn slide is to play tunes you are familiar with. Presented here is a collection of well known traditional, classical, blues, western and popular tunes arranged specifically for slide guitar in standard tuning. Most of the tunes are arranged to keep the melody on one or two strings, so a consistent tone is produced. Some of the tunes have the tablature written down the fretboard to facilitate easier positioning when switching between notes. The tunes are in relative order of difficulty and perfect for those new to slide guitar yet some pieces a decent challenge for intermediate players as well. The added fingerboard charts are a reference for those that prefer to read the notation instead of the tablature. The included slide exercises are helpful for developing slide technique.

Slides

Finding the right slide is a challenge on its own! For many year's slide players would have to conform to commercial slides that are often too big or too narrow. Fortunately, there are many more slide producers now that cater to the different finger sizes and preferred materials. Glass, metal, ceramic, bone, etc. Take the time to experiment and check out different slide manufacturers to get the right fit and material. Of course, this also depends on which finger your wear the slide though there are no rules for this so try different fingers. Most players put the slide on the 3rd or 4th finger as this allows the use of the other fingers to play simultaneously with the slide.   See the "how to play slide" pages that show techniques like "tilt" slide (3) and muting behind the string (4).

Tuning

An important aspect of slide playing is keeping in tune. The note is in tune when placed directly on top and in line with the fret. Though, sometimes the beauty of the slide is to play intentionally "out of tune" producing that slide vibe that is often necessary to the overall sound, particularly when sliding into a note from above or below. Memorizing the tunes in whole or part helps keep your eye on the fingerboard to keep the slide in line with the fret. However, it is also good to practice without looking to develop your sense of touch and sensing the location of your hand and fingers.

Muting

Knowing how to stop the strings ringing is sometimes as important as playing the note. "Muting" is the art of playing slide. The space in between the connecting notes is what you have to focus on. I suggest practicing the exercises and riffs at the back of the book to begin developing this important aspect of slide playing. See the photos in the "how to play" slide pages (1 & 4) to help learn these techniques. Muting technique cannot be underestimated and is essential to good slide playing.

Vibrato

The use of vibrato (move slide quickly back and forth) is not indicated in the music for the reason that vibrato is a personal choice and used where it fits the tune and phrasing according to your playing style and speed. However, most often the vibrato is used on the longer notes. Vibrato can be broken down into two categories: speed and width. The rate of speed your slide moves and the width or distance the slide moves. Experiment with these two techniques to develop your own "style" of playing.

Pressure

Another important aspect of slide playing is how hard you press the slide against the string(s) or referred to as "string pressure". The action (the distance from string to neck) on your guitar determines how hard you will need to press down on the string. Lower actions are tricky as the slide will knock against the frets producing an unwanted buzzing clank that drop and deaden the notes. Most slide players will have a second guitar that has a higher action that is more conducive to slide playing. If you just have one guitar consider raising the action even slightly to get better tone and less fret buzz. For the most part, try and keep a good even pressure on the strings.

Thanks for your purchase and please visit my website for audio tracks at:

www.brentrobitaille.com

http://brentrobitaille.com/guitar

How to Read Guitar Tab

Fingerboard Chart

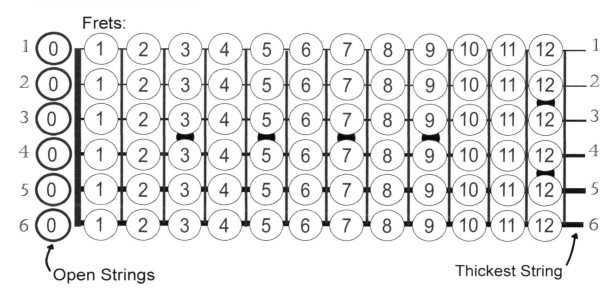

Frets:

Open Strings

Thickest String

Examples

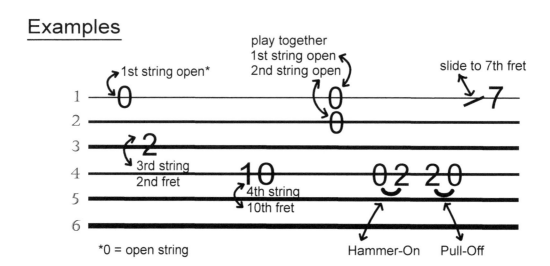

1st string open*

play together
1st string open
2nd string open

slide to 7th fret

3rd string
2nd fret

4th string
10th fret

*0 = open string

Hammer-On

Pull-Off

Slide Notation Guide

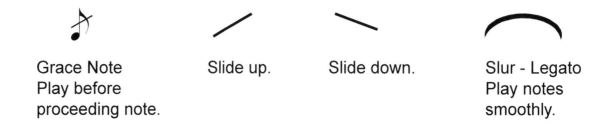

Grace Note
Play before
proceeding note.

Slide up.

Slide down.

Slur - Legato
Play notes
smoothly.

How to Play Slide

1. Place slide directly over top of fret to play note in tune.

2. Place the picking hand finger(s) on strings to stop them from ringing (mute) when the slide sound is not desired.

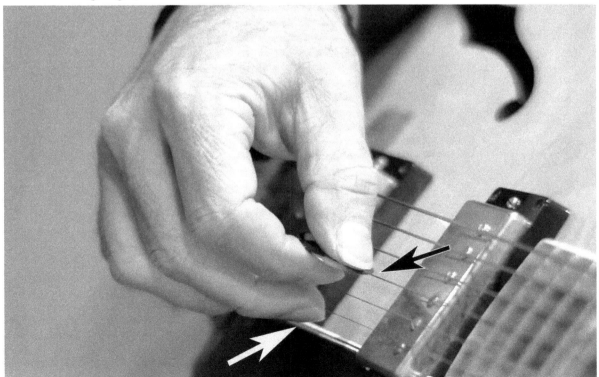

3. Use fingers to play behind or in front of slide by using a "tilt" slide technique.

4. Fretting hand mute is sometimes desired when moving slide. Stop strings with fingers and move hand.

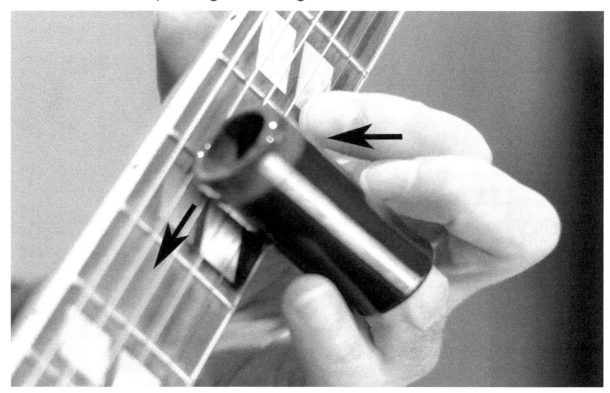

5. Maintain a good even pressure on strings to avoid buzzing.

6. Depress string behind slide with finger and keep slide straight when playing chords.

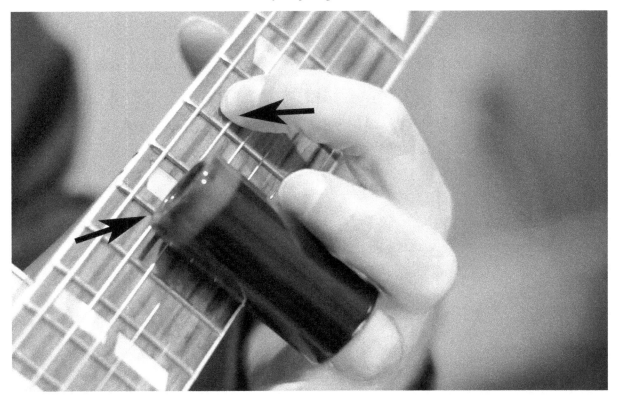

7. Three Points of Vibrato. (1) Thumb acts as a pivot.

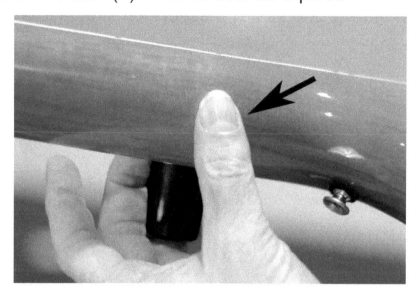

(2) Place slide in line with fret and move from side to side.

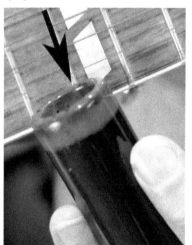  

(3) Loose Wrist. Focus on moving wrist back and forth.

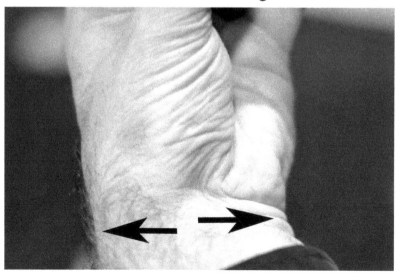

House of the Rising Sun

Traditional

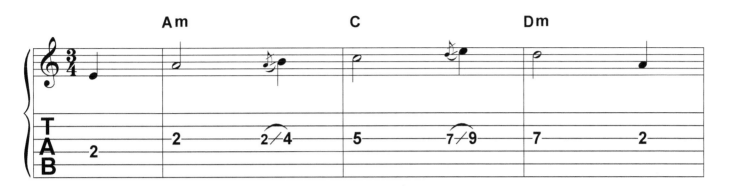

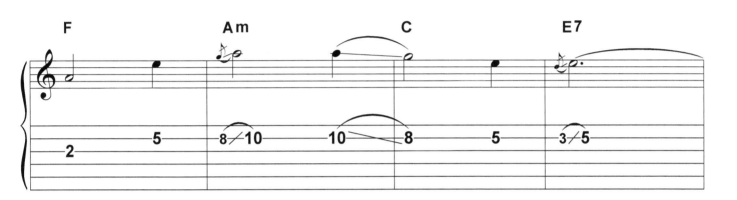

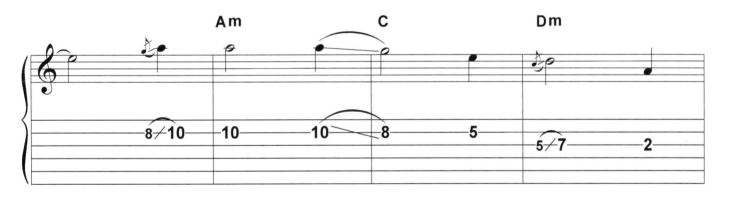

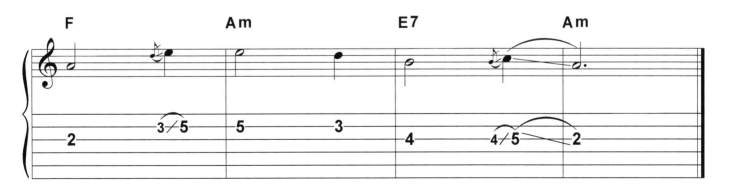

Scarborough Fair

English Ballad

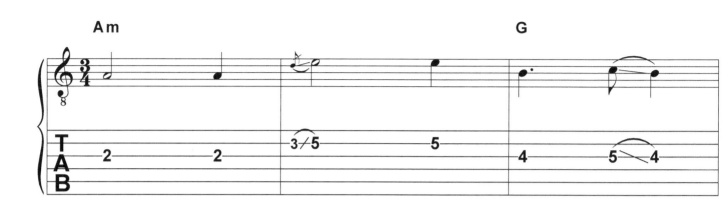

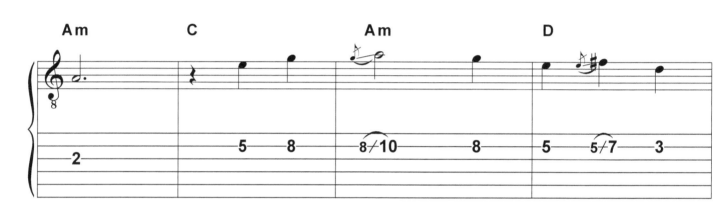

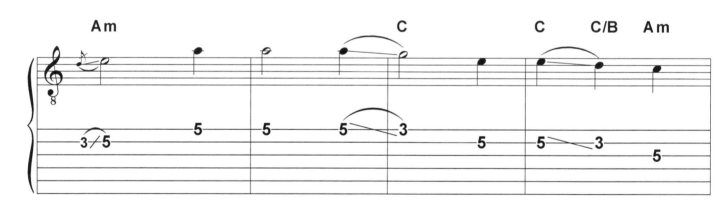

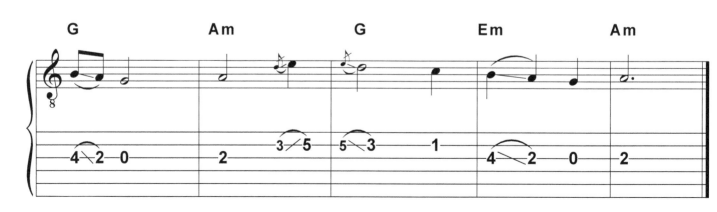

The Water is Wide

Folk Song

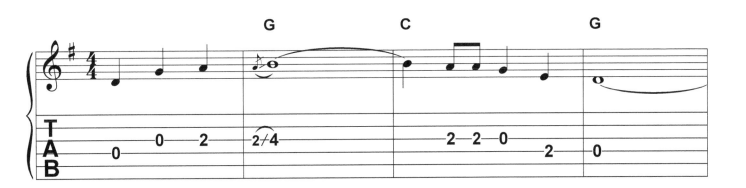

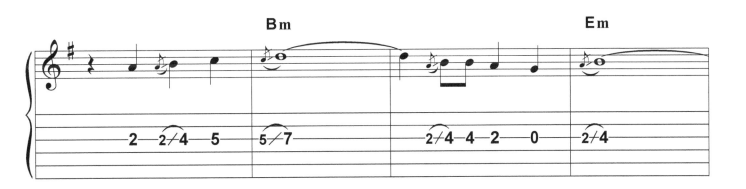

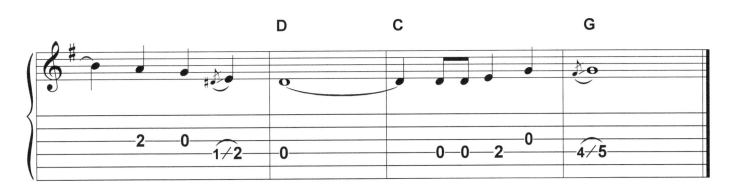

Be Thou My Vision

Traditional

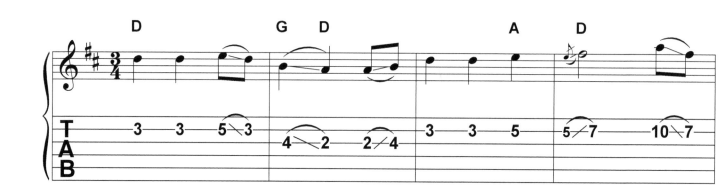

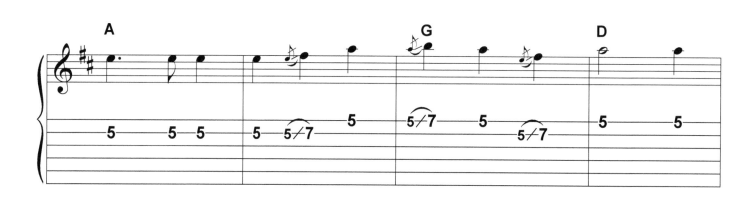

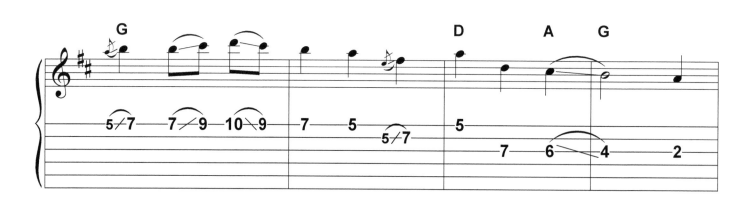

Shenandoah

American Folk Song

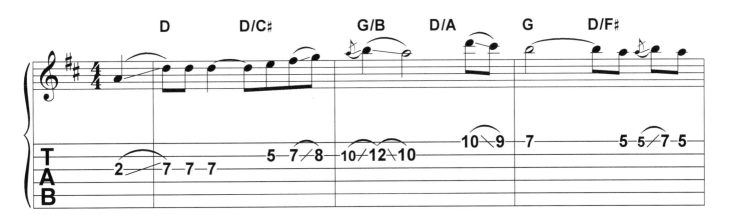

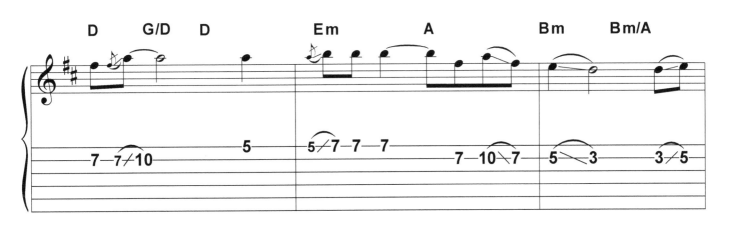

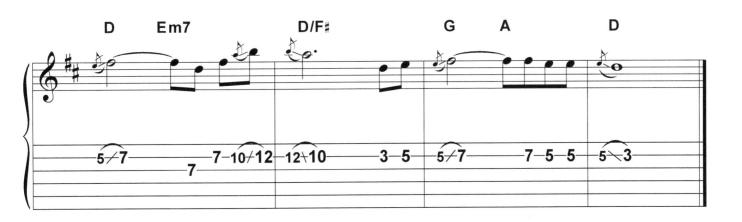

Worried Man Blues

Folk Song

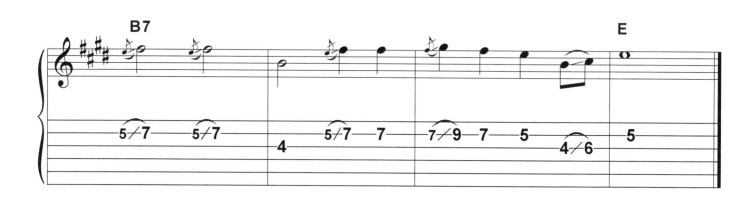

Ode to Joy

Beethoven

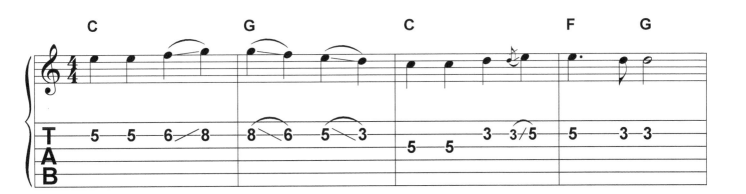

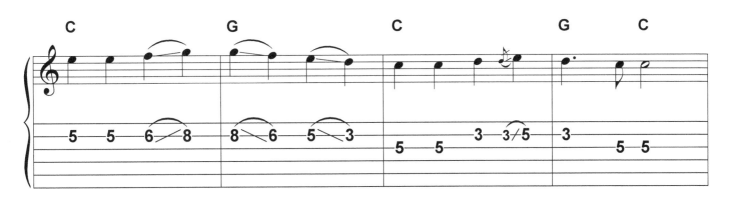

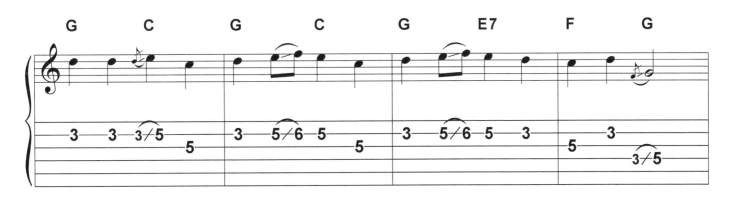

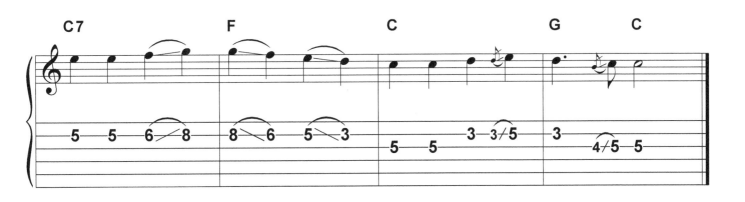

Little Brown Jug

Popular Song

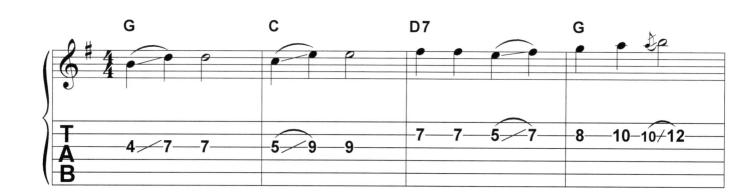

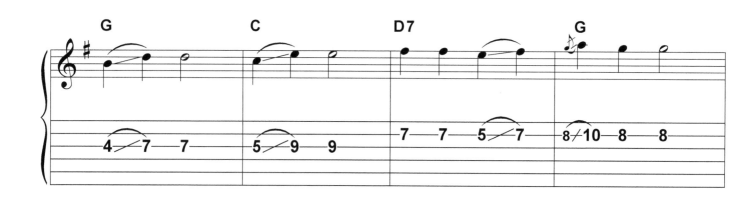

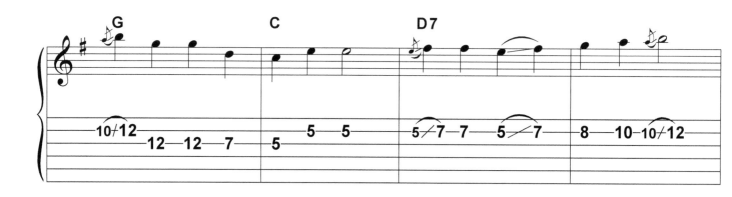

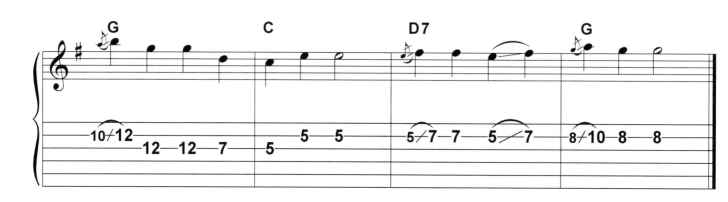

When the Saints Go Marching In

Gospel

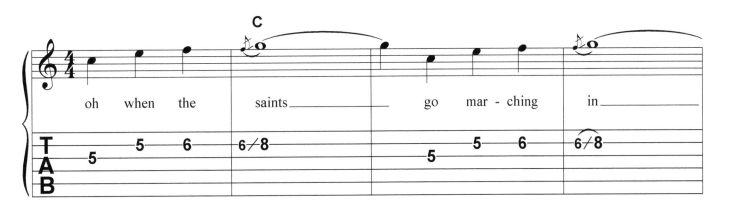

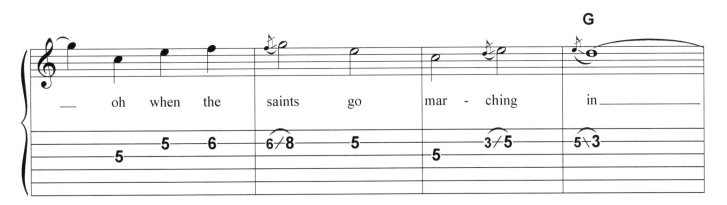

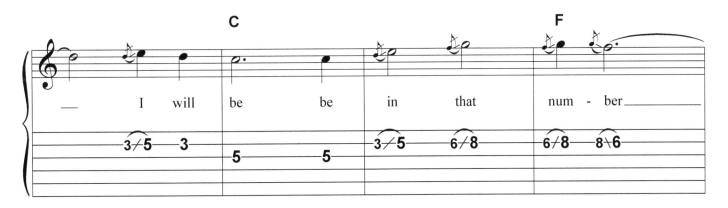

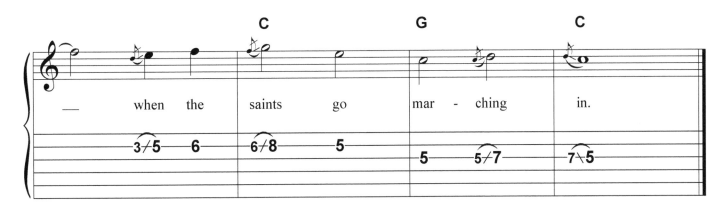

Greensleeves

English Folk Song

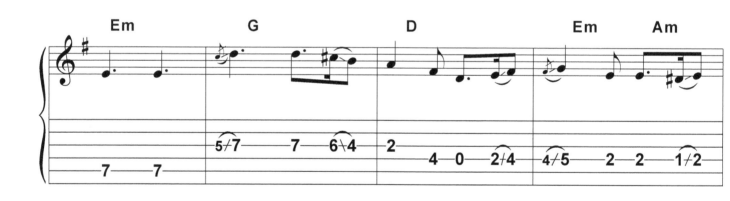

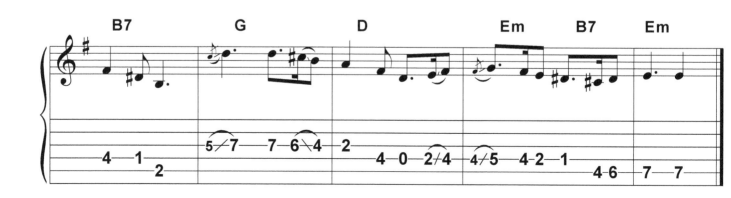

Will the Circle Be Unbroken

Traditional Hymn

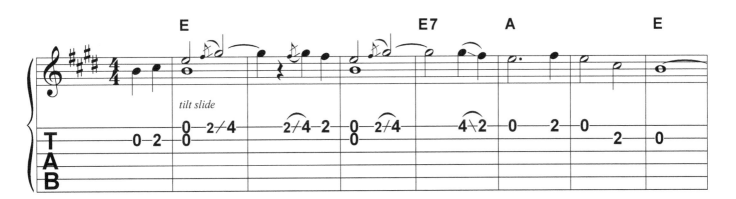

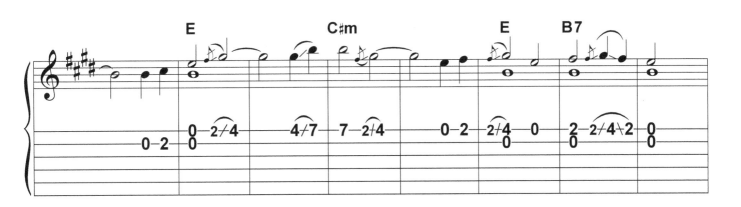

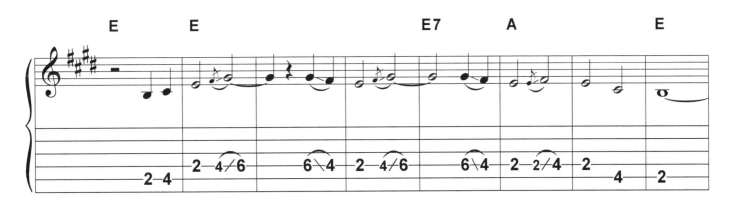

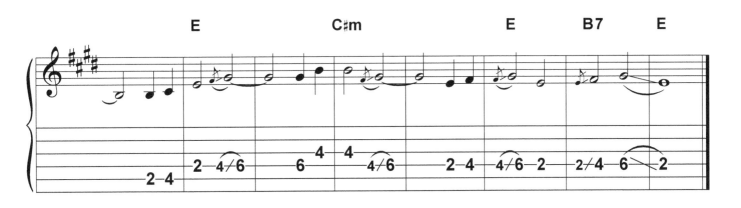

Wild Mountain Thyme

Folk Song

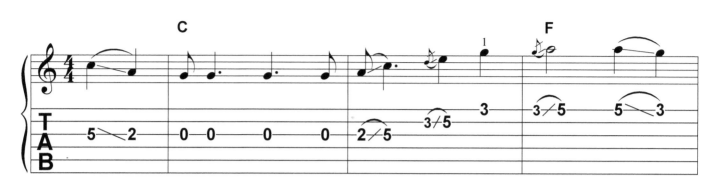

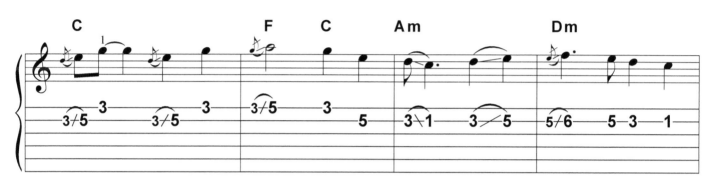

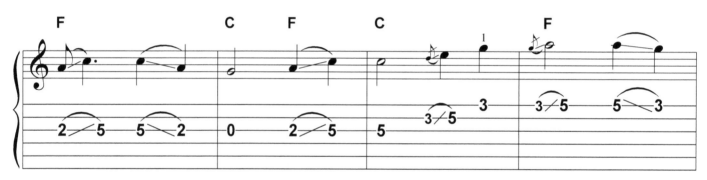

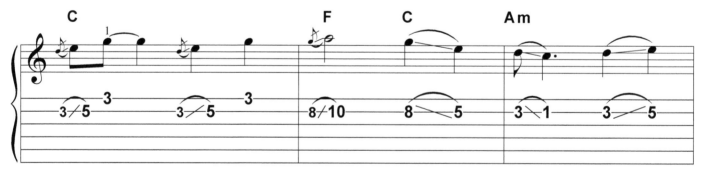

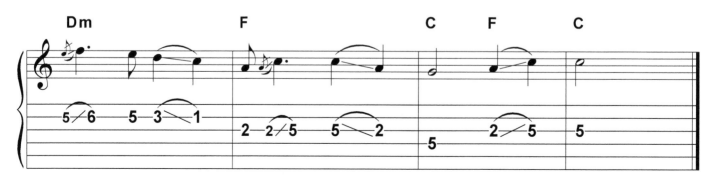

Wayfaring Stranger

Traditional Song

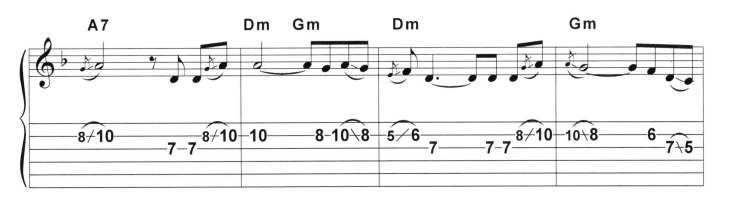

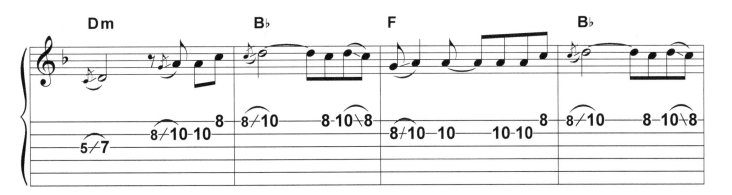

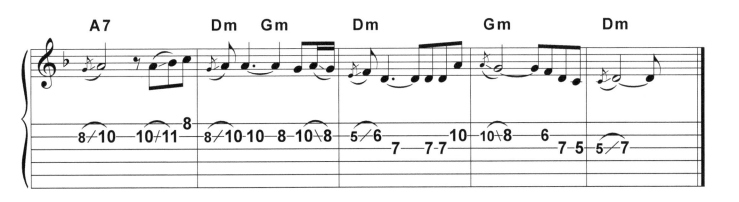

Skye Boat Song

Scottish Folk Song

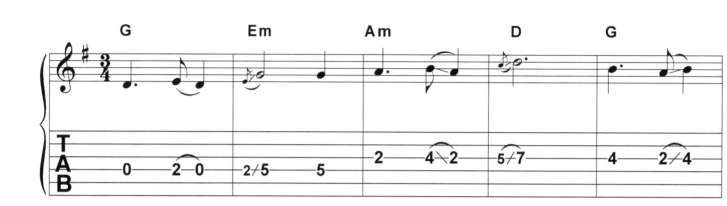

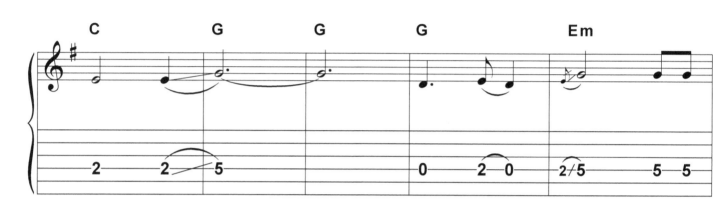

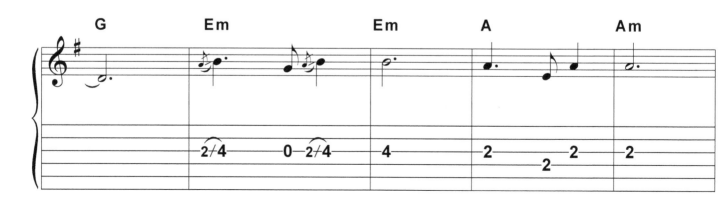

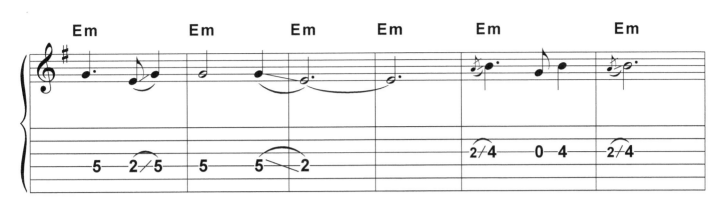

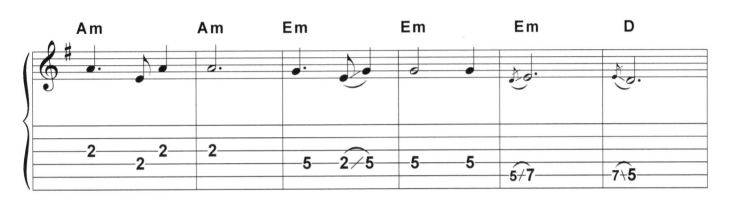

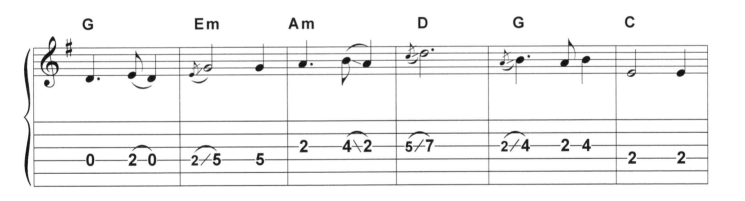

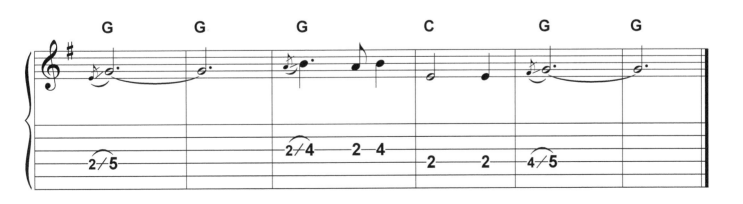

Amazing Grace

Hymn

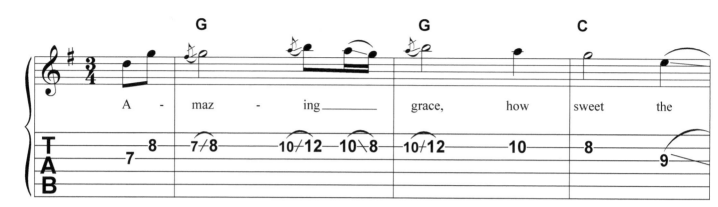

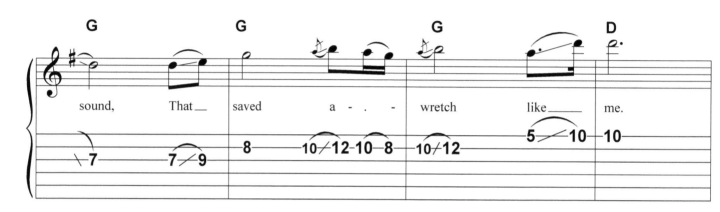

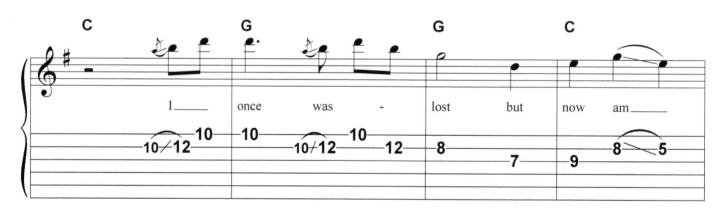

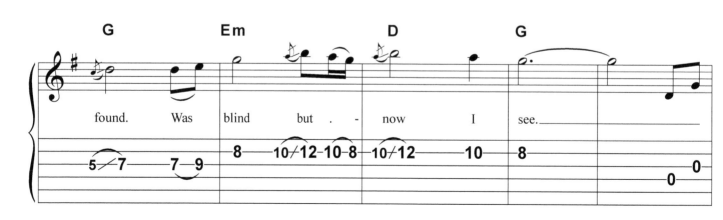

Amazing Grace - 2

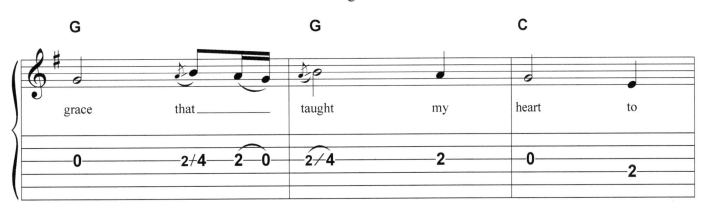

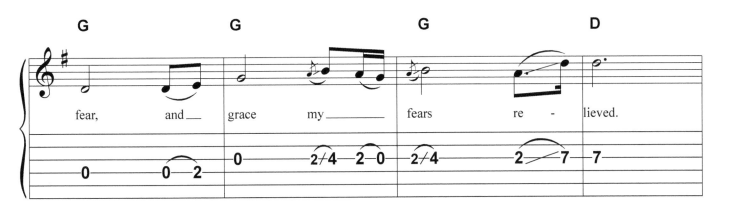

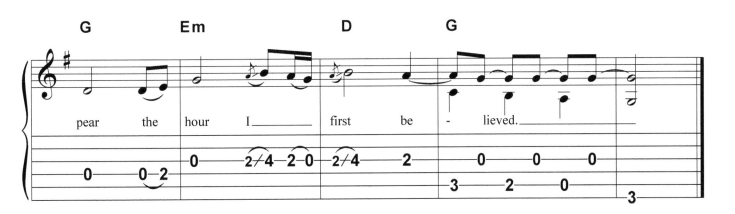

The Parting Glass

Traditonal Song

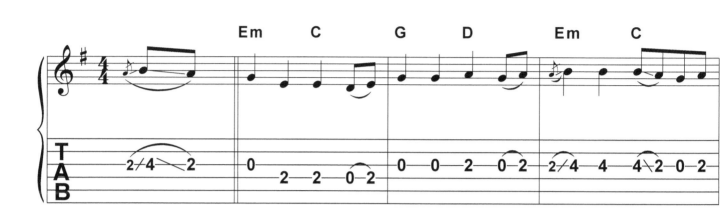

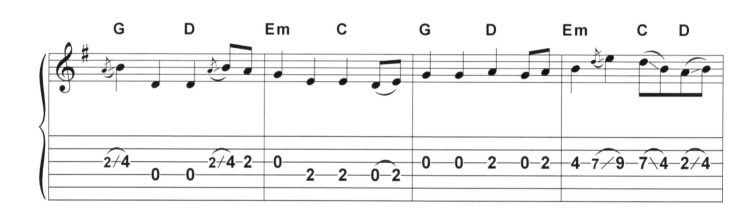

The Parting Glass - 2

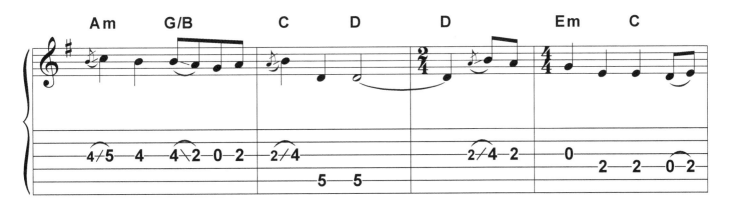

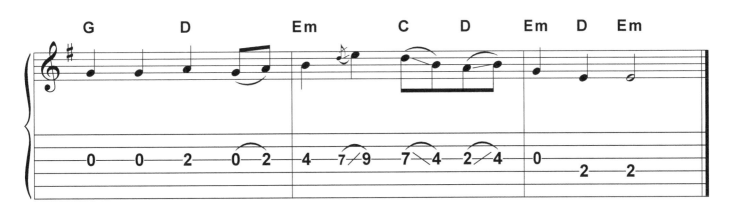

Danny Boy

Folk Song

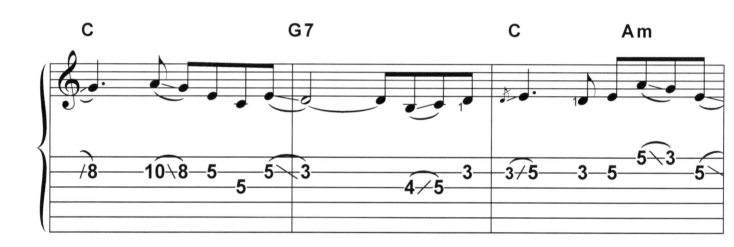

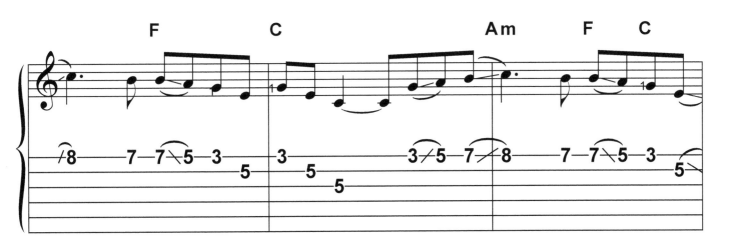

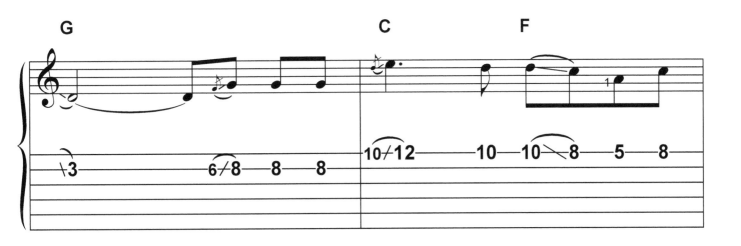

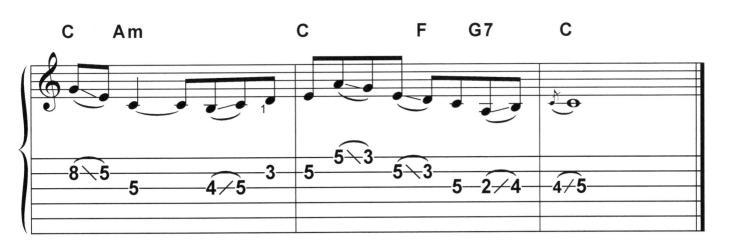

Fur Elise

Beethoven

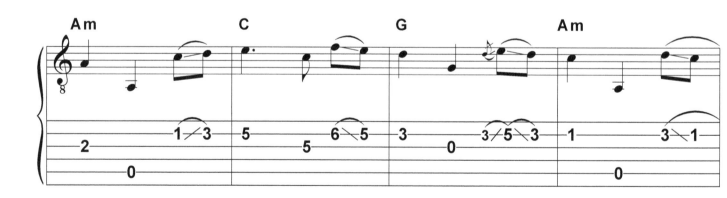

Streets of Laredo

Cowboy Ballad

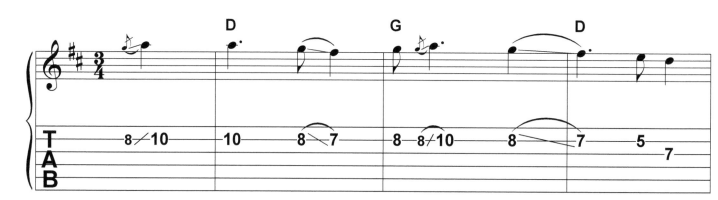

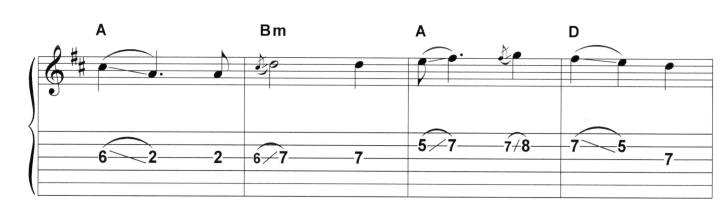

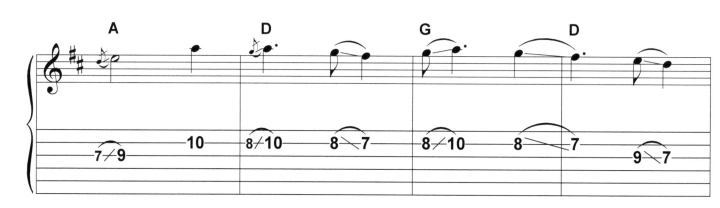

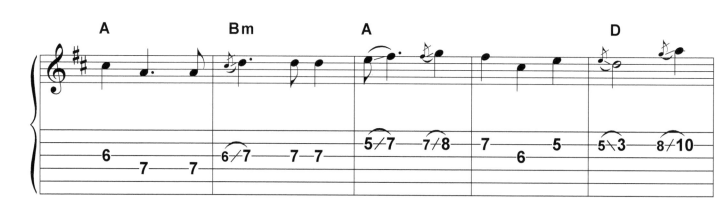

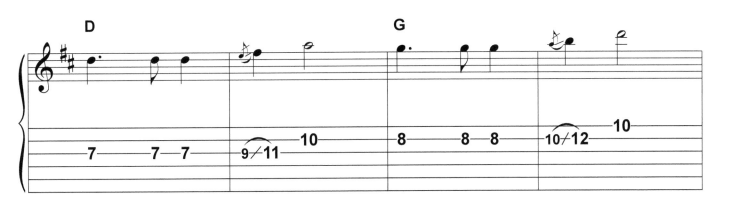

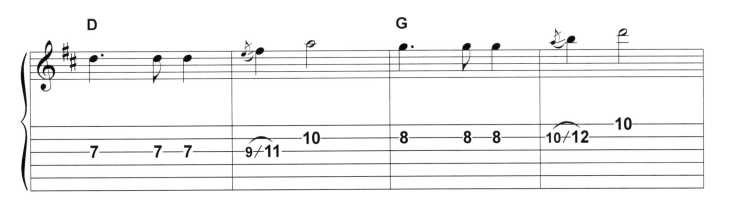
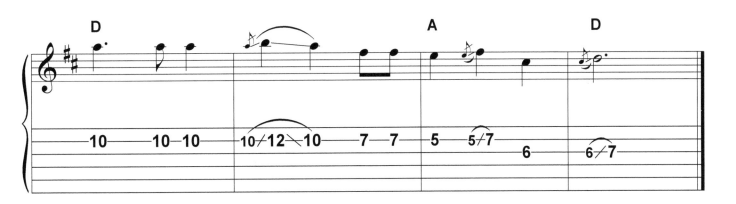

Bill Bailey, Won't You Please Come Home

Hughie Cannon

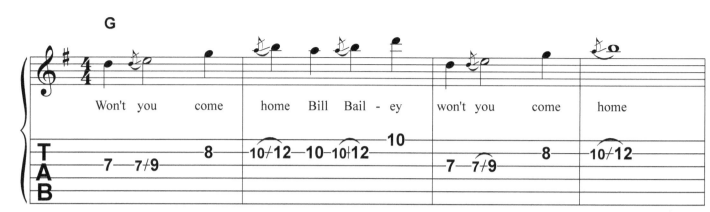

Won't you come home Bill Bail - ey won't you come home

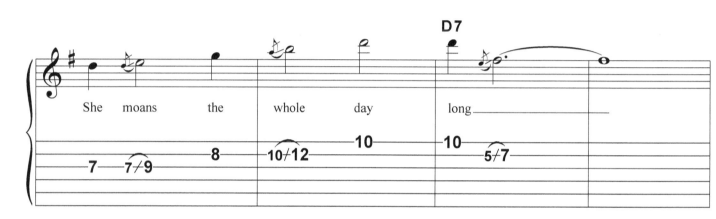

She moans the whole day long

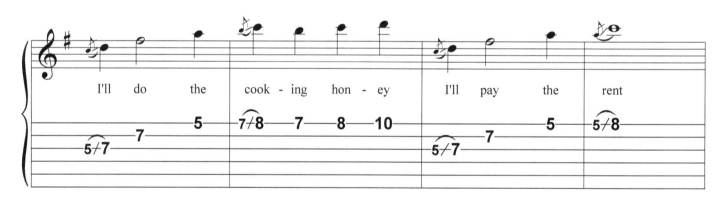

I'll do the cook - ing hon - ey I'll pay the rent

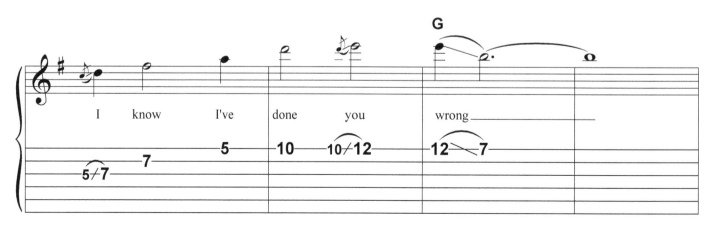

I know I've done you wrong

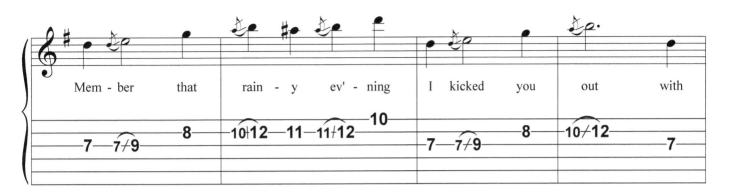

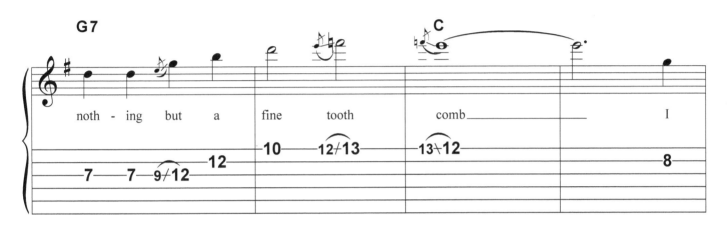

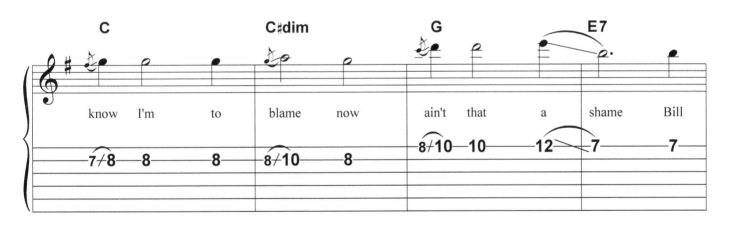

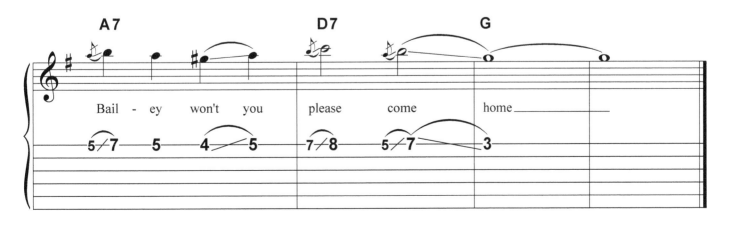

Saint Louis Blues

W.C. Handy

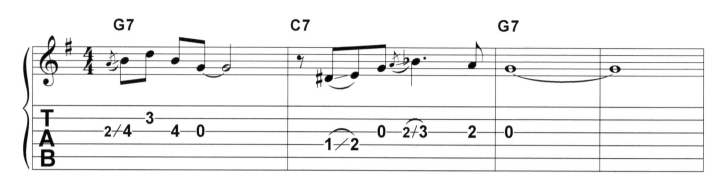

Saint Louis Blues - 2

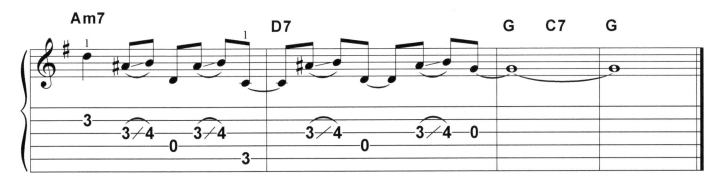

The Blue Danube

Johann Strauss

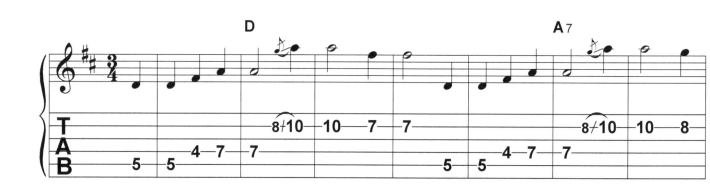

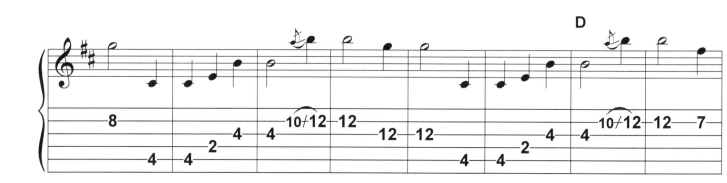

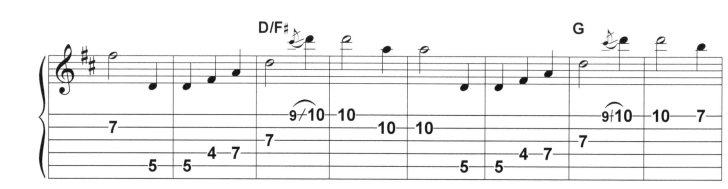

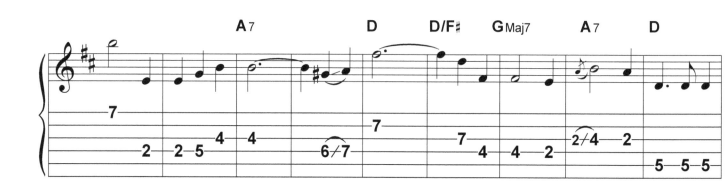

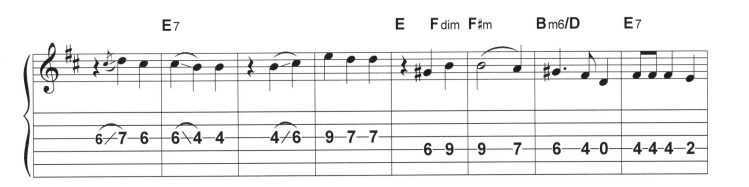

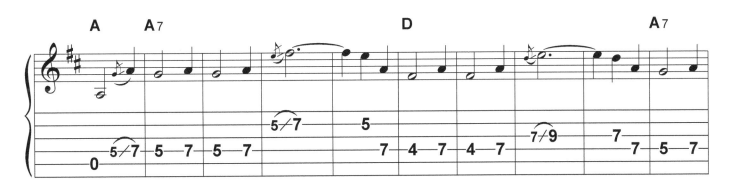

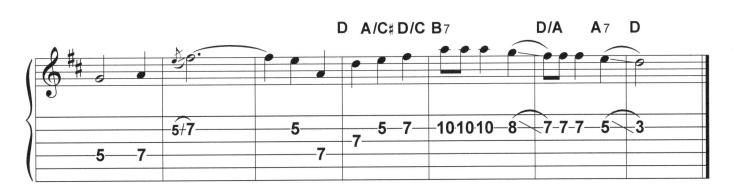

After You've Gone

Creamer & Layton

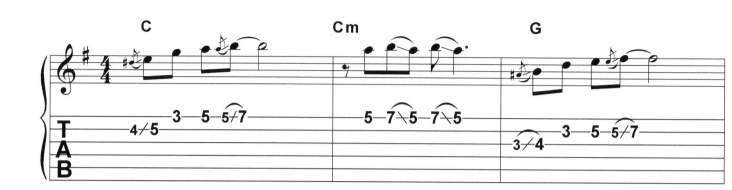

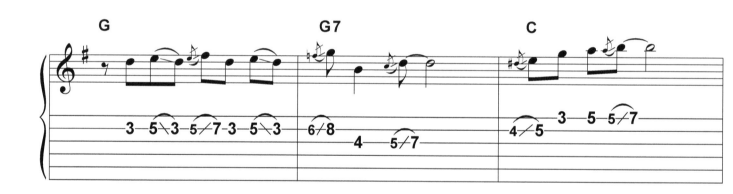

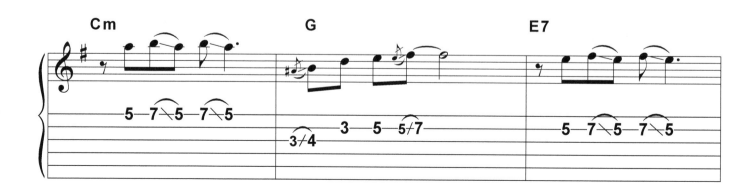

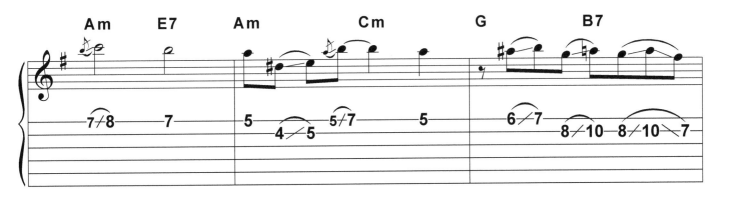

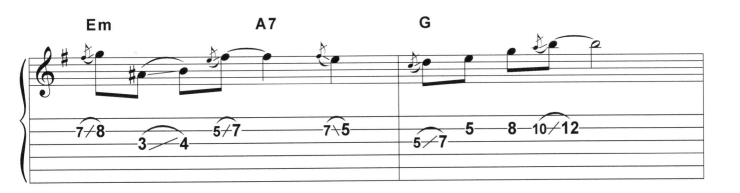

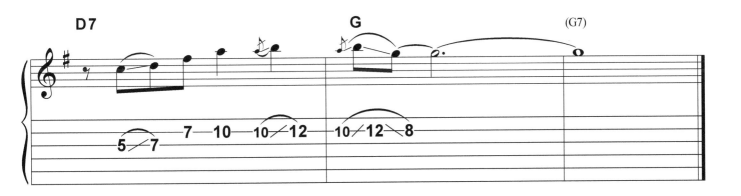

Beale Street Blues

W.C. Handy

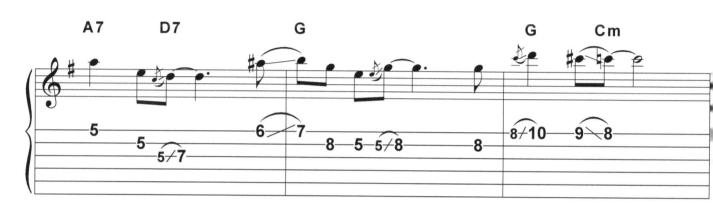

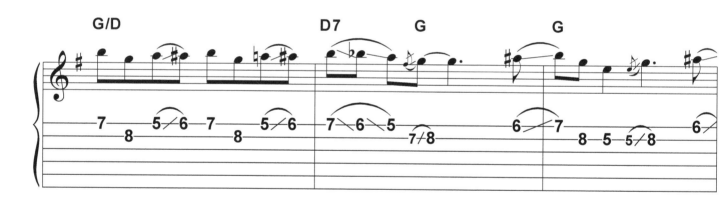

Beale Street Blues -2

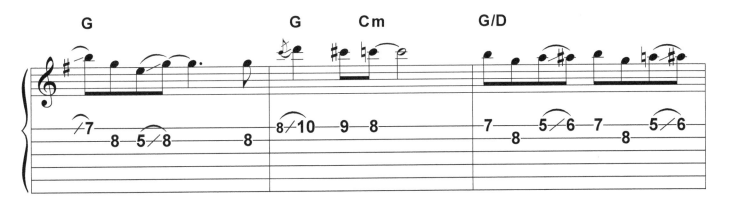

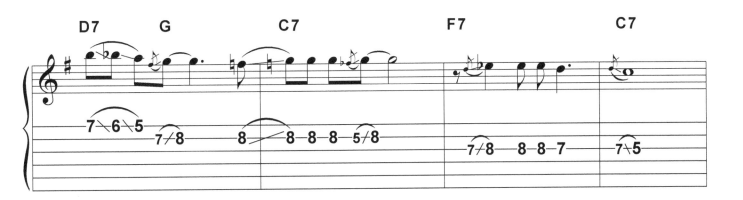

Air on the G String

J.S. Bach

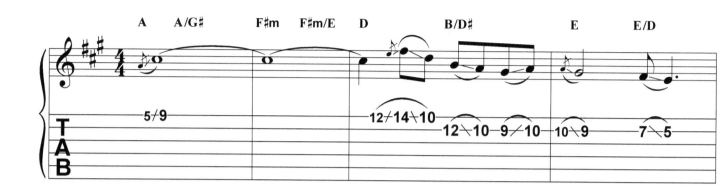

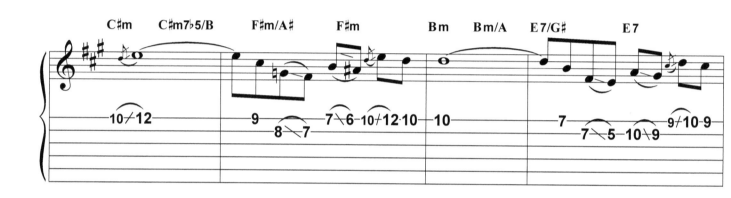

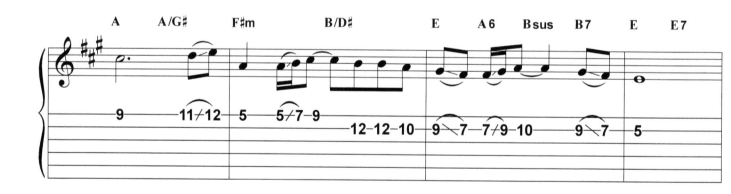

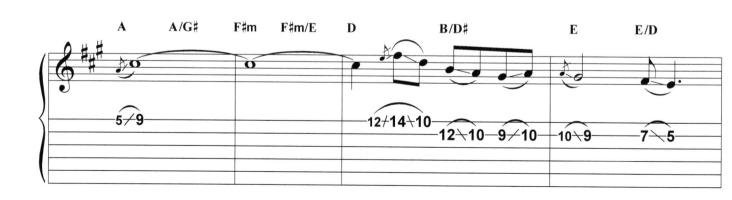

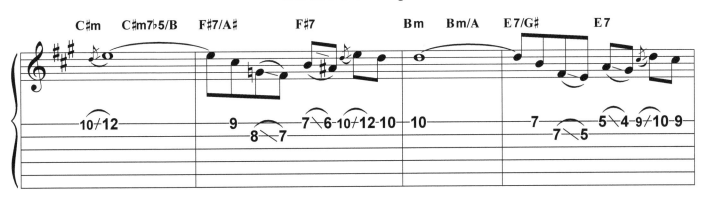

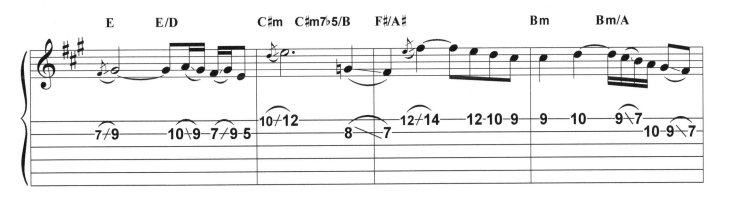

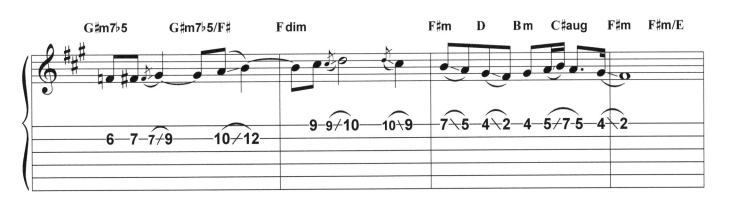

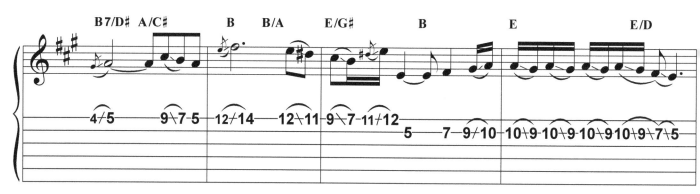

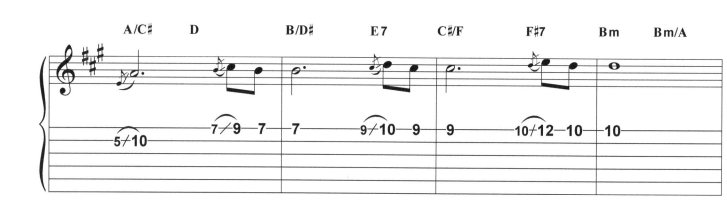

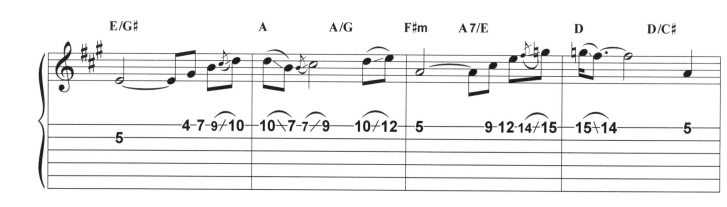

Slide Guitar Exercises

① *Muting Exercise. Repeat this scale on all 6 strings. Play note - Mute string - Move slide silently.*

② *Arpeggio Exercise. Play - Mute - Move*

③ *Pitch Exercise. Repeat this on all strings. Place slide directly over fret to play in tune.*

④ *Slide - Mute - Play with First Finger.*

5 *Tilt Slide - 3rd's Exercise. Play 3rd string with slide and 2nd string with finger.*

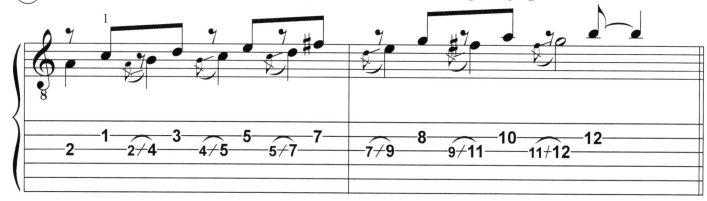

6 *Tilt Slide 6th's Exercise. Play 4th string with slide and 2nd string with finger.*

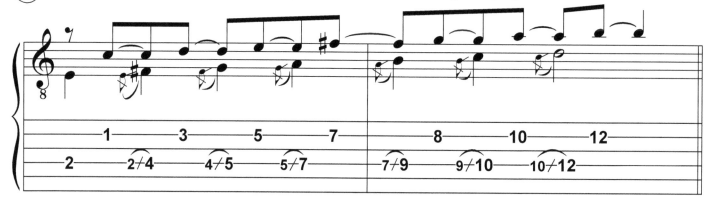

7 *Tilt Slide Boogie Blues Exercise.*

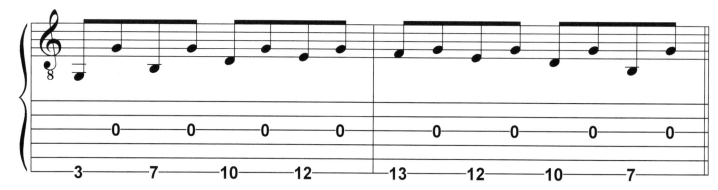

8 *Pull-off Exercise. Play first note (3 fret) then pull off slide without plucking string again.*

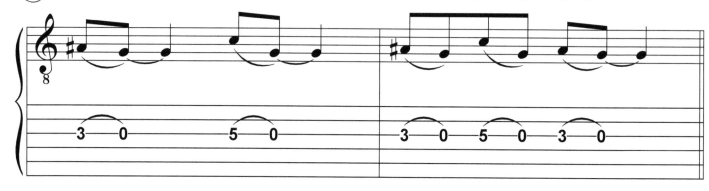

9 *Hammer-On Exercise. Play first note open then hammer down slide without plucking 2nd note.*

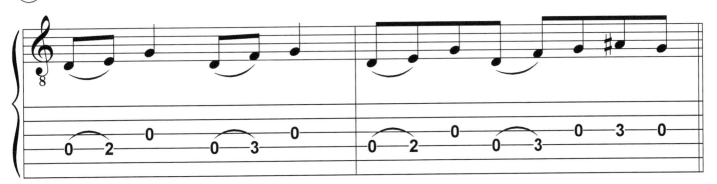

10 *Chord Exercise. Lay slide straight over 3 frets - play 1st finger on 5th string.*

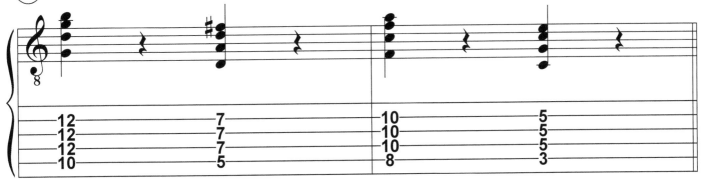

11 *Minor Major Chord Slide Exercise. Tilt slide to play 2nd string with 1st finger (minor chords only).*

12 *Pedal Steel Lick - Tilt Slide then hammer-on. Keep slide down so all notes ring.*

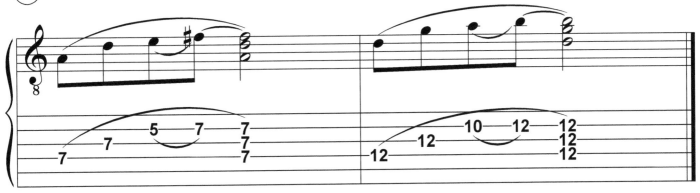

Guitar Note Chart

1st String - E

E	F	F#	Gb	G	G#	Ab	A	A#	Bb	B	C	C#	Db	D	D#	Eb	E	F	F#	Gb	G
0	1	2	2	3	4	4	5	6	6	7	8	9	9	10	11	11	12	13	14	14	15

2nd String - B

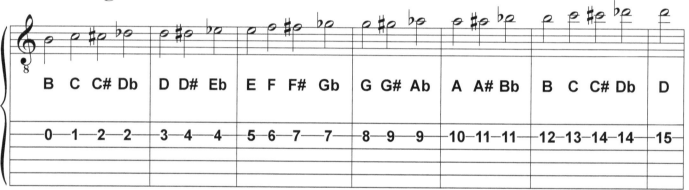

B	C	C#	Db	D	D#	Eb	E	F	F#	Gb	G	G#	Ab	A	A#	Bb	B	C	C#	Db	D
0	1	2	2	3	4	4	5	6	7	7	8	9	9	10	11	11	12	13	14	14	15

3rd String - G

G	G#	Ab	A	A#	Bb	B	C	C#	Db	D	D#	Eb	E	F	F#	Gb	G	G#	Ab	A	A#	Bb
0	1	1	2	3	3	4	5	6	6	7	8	8	9	10	11	11	12	13	13	14	15	15

4th String - D

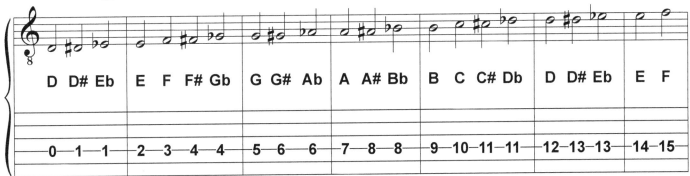

5th String - A

6th String - E

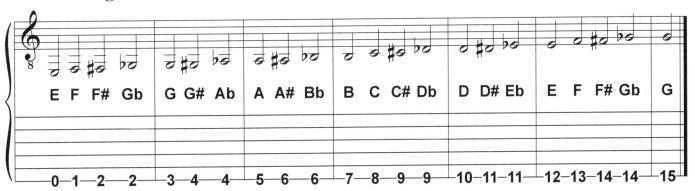

Guitar Fingerboard

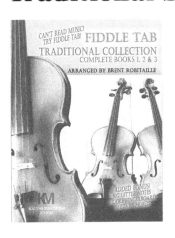

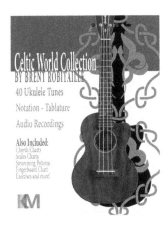
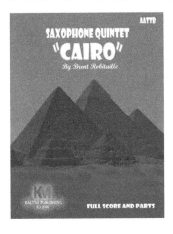

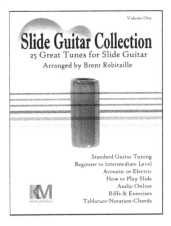
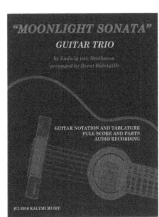

CPSIA information can be obtained
at www.ICGtesting.com
Printed in the USA
LVHW101102140119
603814LV00018B/436/P